DO YOU BELIEVE?
BERMUDA TRIANGLE

by Natalie Deniston

Ideas for Parents and Teachers

Pogo Books let children practice reading informational text while introducing them to nonfiction features such as headings, labels, sidebars, maps, and diagrams, as well as a table of contents, glossary, and index.

Carefully leveled text with a strong photo match offers early fluent readers the support they need to succeed.

Before Reading

- "Walk" through the book and point out the various nonfiction features. Ask the student what purpose each feature serves.
- Look at the glossary together. Read and discuss the words.

Read the Book

- Have the child read the book independently.
- Invite him or her to list questions that arise from reading.

After Reading

- Discuss the child's questions. Talk about how he or she might find answers to those questions.
- Prompt the child to think more. Ask: Do you think there is something strange about the Bermuda Triangle? Why or why not?

Pogo Books are published by Jump!
5357 Penn Avenue South
Minneapolis, MN 55419
www.jumplibrary.com

Copyright © 2025 Jump!
International copyright reserved in all countries. No part of this book may be reproduced in any form without written permission from the publisher.

Library of Congress Cataloging-in-Publication Data

Names: Deniston, Natalie, author.
Title: Bermuda Triangle / by Natalie Deniston.
Description: Minneapolis, MN: Jump!, Inc., [2025]
Series: Do you believe? | Includes index.
Audience: Ages 7-10
Identifiers: LCCN 2023056814 (print)
LCCN 2023056815 (ebook)
ISBN 9798892132213 (hardcover)
ISBN 9798892132220 (paperback)
ISBN 9798892132237 (ebook)
Subjects: LCSH: Bermuda Triangle—Juvenile literature. Disappearances (Parapsychology)—Bermuda Triangle—Juvenile literature. | Curiosities and wonders—Juvenile literature.
Classification: LCC G558 .D48 2025 (print)
LCC G558 (ebook)
DDC 001.94—dc23/eng/20231208
LC record available at https://lccn.loc.gov/2023056814
LC ebook record available at https://lccn.loc.gov/2023056815

Editor: Jenna Gleisner
Designer: Emma Almgren-Bersie

Photo Credits: Anton Balazh/Shutterstock, cover; Oskari Porkka/Shutterstock, 1; Pseudopanax/Wikimedia, 3; ESB Professional/Shutterstock, 4; Ftiare/Shutterstock, 5; CaraMaria/iStock, 6-7; Michael Rosskothen/Shutterstock, 8; Album/Alamy, 9; U.S. Naval History and Heritage Command, 10-11, 14-15; jcrosemann/iStock, 12-13; Harvepino/Shutterstock, 16-17; Siberian Art/Shutterstock, 18; Stockbym/Shutterstock, 19; MikeMareen/iStock, 20-21; PTZ Pictures/Shutterstock, 23.

Printed in the United States of America at Corporate Graphics in North Mankato, Minnesota.

TABLE OF CONTENTS

CHAPTER 1
Lost in the Atlantic...4

CHAPTER 2
Mysteries in the Sea and Sky...................8

CHAPTER 3
Bermuda Triangle Theories....................18

QUICK FACTS & TOOLS
Timeline...22
Glossary..23
Index...24
To Learn More..24

CHAPTER 1

LOST IN THE ATLANTIC

Off the coast of Bermuda is a mysterious spot. It is called the Bermuda Triangle. People say strange things happen in this area of the Atlantic Ocean. Like what?

Ships disappear. They are never found again. Airplanes **vanish** from the sky. The weather here can be dangerous.

CHAPTER 1

The Triangle stretches from Bermuda to Florida to Puerto Rico. This area is busy. Why? People travel through daily. Some are never heard from again.

TAKE A LOOK!

Where is the Bermuda Triangle? Take a look!

CHAPTER 2
MYSTERIES IN THE SEA AND SKY

Mysterious things have happened here for hundreds of years. One of the earliest stories is from 1492. Christopher Columbus was an **explorer**. He sailed in the Triangle.

One night, Columbus saw fire in the sky. He said it crashed into the sea. He also said he saw strange lights in the sky. **Compasses** stopped working. They did not point north. Why? Nobody could explain.

compass

CHAPTER 2

In February 1918, the USS *Cyclops* left Brazil. It was a **cargo** ship. It was going through the Triangle on its way to Maryland. The ship was supposed to arrive March 13. But it never did.

WHAT DO YOU THINK?

The Bermuda Triangle has many names. One is "The Devil's Triangle." Why do you think some people call it that?

CHAPTER 2

The ship was never found. The crew never sent an **S.O.S.** call. Later, the ship was **declared** lost. The 306 people on board were believed to be dead.

What happened? No one knows. The cargo on the ship was very heavy. The ship sat low in the water. If a big storm came, maybe waves sank the ship. Or maybe the Triangle made it disappear.

WHAT DO YOU THINK?

Nobody knows what happened to the USS *Cyclops*. What do you think happened?

CHAPTER 2

On December 5, 1945, five U.S. Navy airplanes left Florida. This group became known as Flight 19. They were scheduled to fly to an area called Hen and Chicken Shoals. Then they would fly to the Bahamas and back to Florida.

CHAPTER 2

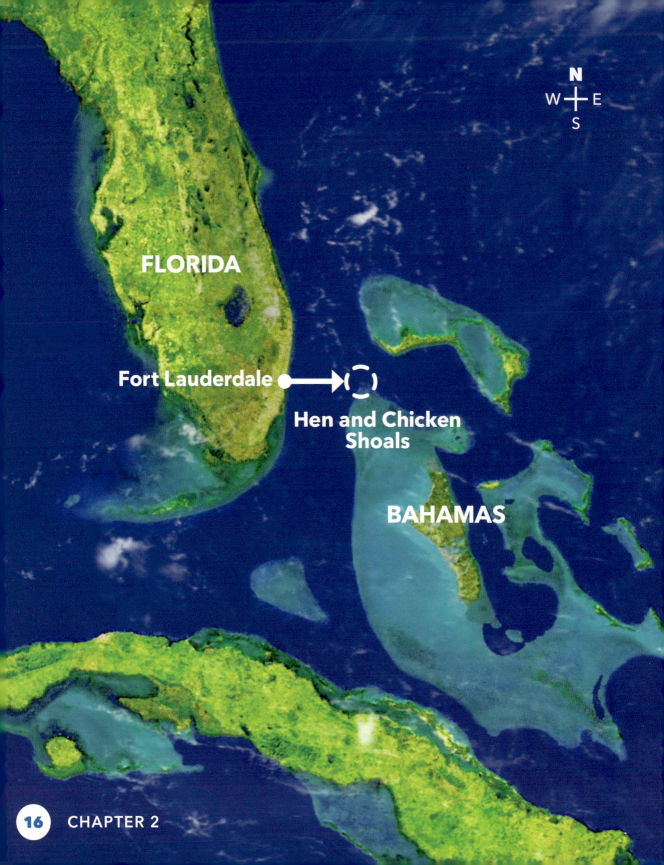

Something went wrong. Charles C. Taylor led the group. His compasses stopped working. He radioed for help.

The sun went down. The weather turned stormy. The planes were low on fuel. Rescuers searched for them. But no sign of Flight 19 was ever found.

DID YOU KNOW?

During the search, one of the rescue planes exploded in the air. Six planes were lost. In total, 27 people died.

CHAPTER 2

CHAPTER 3
BERMUDA TRIANGLE THEORIES

What happens in the Triangle? There are many **theories**. A **magnetic field** surrounds Earth. It makes compasses point north. But there are places this doesn't work well. One is the Triangle. Travelers can get lost.

magnetic field

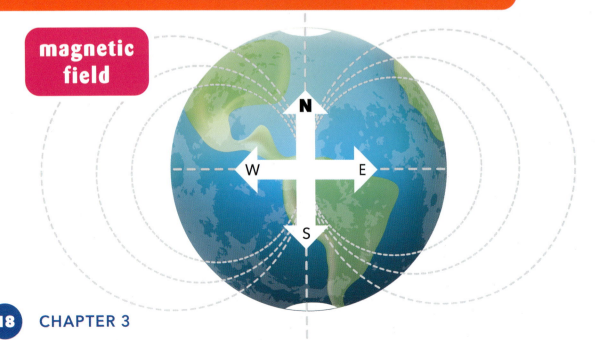

Some people believe **aliens** are to blame. They say aliens steal planes and ships in the Triangle. Others think **Atlantis** was once there. They believe it sank into the Atlantic Ocean. Could it affect ships or airplanes?

Atlantis

CHAPTER 3

The Atlantic Ocean has many **hurricanes**. Large **rogue waves** form. Storms and large waves can tip ships.

Many people say the Bermuda Triangle is no different than the rest of the ocean. What do you believe?

CHAPTER 3

QUICK FACTS & TOOLS

TIMELINE

Mysterious things have happened in the Bermuda Triangle for thousands of years. Take a look!

360 BCE
Greek philosopher Plato writes about Atlantis. Some people today believe it is in the Bermuda Triangle.

1492
Christopher Columbus sees strange lights in the sky while sailing through the Triangle.

MARCH 1918
The USS *Cyclops* disappears in the Triangle. More than 300 people go missing and are never found.

DECEMBER 5, 1945
Five U.S. Navy planes disappear during a training exercise. A search and rescue plane explodes. In all, 27 people die.

1974
Charles Berlitz writes *The Bermuda Triangle*. The book spreads the legend of the Triangle.

2024
It is believed more than 50 ships and 20 airplanes have disappeared in the Triangle.

GLOSSARY

aliens: Creatures from other planets.

Atlantis: A mythical lost island first written about by the ancient Greek philosopher Plato.

cargo: Goods carried to a place in a ship, airplane, or other vehicle.

compasses: Devices used for navigation that work by using magnets to point north.

declared: Announced something officially.

explorer: Someone who travels to discover new places or information.

hurricanes: Violent storms with heavy rain and high winds.

magnetic field: An area surrounding Earth that has magnetic force.

rogue waves: Unpredictable, large waves that often come in different directions than the wind and other waves.

S.O.S.: A code used by ships and airplanes to call for help in emergencies.

theories: Ideas or opinions that are based on some facts or evidence but are not proven.

vanish: To disappear suddenly.

QUICK FACTS & TOOLS

INDEX

airplanes 5, 14, 17, 19
aliens 19
Atlantic Ocean 4, 7, 19, 20
Atlantis 19
Bahamas 7, 14, 16
Bermuda 4, 6, 7
cargo 11, 12
Columbus, Christopher 8, 9
compasses 9, 17, 18
disappear 5, 12
Flight 19 14, 17

Florida 6, 7, 14, 16
Hen and Chicken Shoals 14, 16
hurricanes 20
magnetic field 18
Puerto Rico 6, 7
rogue waves 20
ships 5, 11, 12, 19, 20
S.O.S. call 12
Taylor, Charles C. 17
theories 18
USS *Cyclops* 11, 12

TO LEARN MORE

Finding more information is as easy as 1, 2, 3.

1. Go to www.factsurfer.com
2. Enter "BermudaTriangle" into the search box.
3. Choose your book to see a list of websites.

24 QUICK FACTS & TOOLS